A PICTURE OF GOD

3 in 1

WRITTEN BY JOANNE MARXHAUSEN

PICTURES BY BEN MARXHAUSEN AND ED KOEHLER

CONCORDIA PUBLISHING HOUSE · SAINT LOUIS

Here is **1** apple.

There is only **1** true God.

The apple has three parts:

The peel.

The flesh.

The core.

The 1 true God has three Persons:

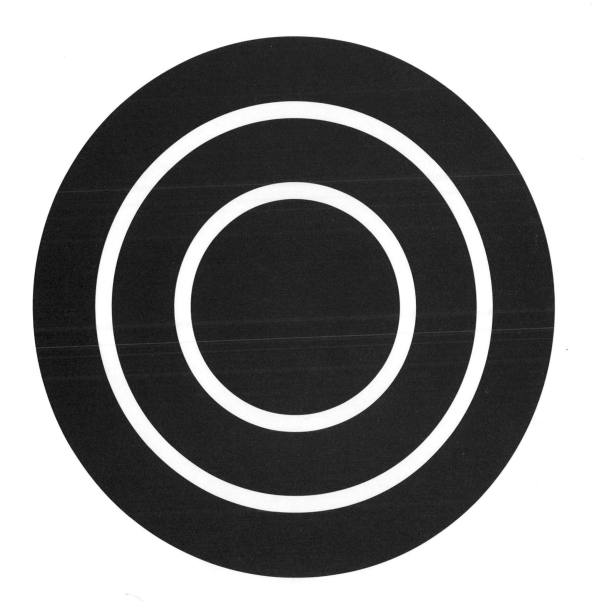

God the Father.

God the Son.

God the Holy Spirit.

All three parts

of the apple are _____ apple.

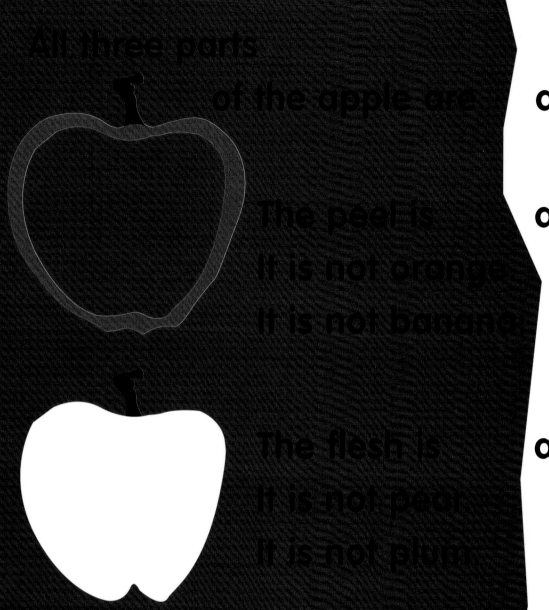

The peel is _____ apple.

It is not orange.

It is not banana.

The flesh is _____ apple.

It is not pear.

It is not plum.

The core is _____ apple.

It is not grapefruit.

It is not watermelon.

But these three:

Peel

Flesh

Core

Are not three apples

But just  apple.

All three Persons of the 1 true God are God.

But these three:

Father

Son

Holy Spirit

Are not three gods

But just 1 God.

The three parts of the apple
have different purposes.

The peel protects.

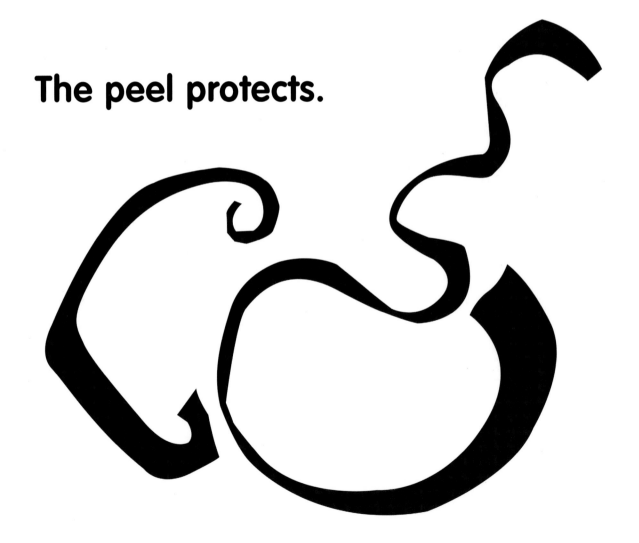

It keeps the apple healthy.

The flesh of the apple
is good to eat.

Lots of good things to eat are made from the flesh of the apple.

Apple pie

Apple crisp

Apple sauce

Apple cider

Apple dumplings

Apple jelly

Applesauce cake

Apple fritters

The core of the apple
contains seeds from which
apple trees grow.

Many, many apples.

Like the apple,
the three Persons of the 1 true God
have different purposes.

God the Father

is our Protector.

He made us –

You
Me
All people
All things
Even apples

He loves us and protects us, makes even bad things turn out for our good.

He keeps things growing so we have food –

Cows
Carrots
Even apples

Sometimes we do things
that God doesn't like.

God said there must be a
punishment for these things.

That would
make us
very sad.

It would
hurt a lot

For a very
long, long
time.

But God loves us so much
He sent

God the Son

To take our punishment for us.

His name is
Jesus

He was
a real man.

He suffered.

It hurt a lot.

He died.

Jesus was buried
as an apple seed is buried
in the ground.

**But He was really God
and as an apple seed sprouts from the
ground and makes new apples possible,**

**Jesus rose
from the dead**

Beautiful,

wonderful,

happy new lives for us.

But before we can have this

Beautiful

Wonderful

Happiness

There is
something else
we must have –

Faith n Jesus...

When you plant an apple seed
in the ground, you believe an apple tree
will grow from it.

That's faith
in an apple seed.

When you believe
Jesus died for you and lives again
to give you a beautiful,
wonderful,
happy new life,

That's faith
in Jesus.

Our hearts are like a piece of ground.

We cannot put faith into our own hearts.

God the Holy Spirit

makes us believe in Jesus.

He puts faith
into our hearts

and keeps it
alive and growing

as long as we
want Him to.

When
an
apple
seed
is
planted
in
the
ground,
the
rain
feeds
it,
and
it
begins
to
grow.

When the Holy Spirit puts faith
into the heart,
He feeds it with God's Word,

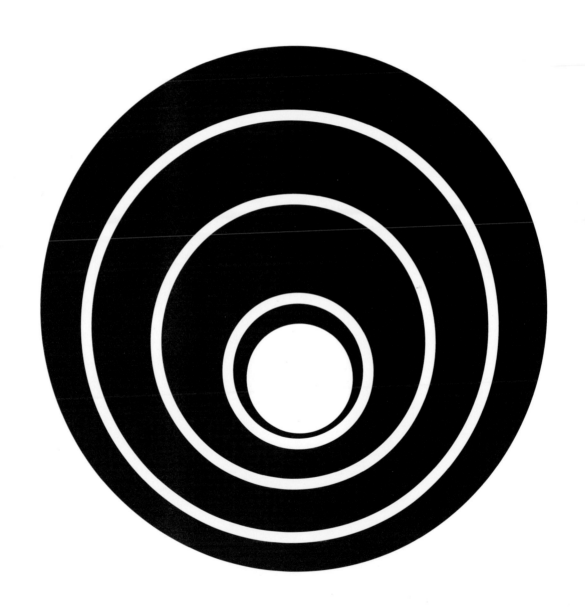

and faith begins to grow.

When the apple
tree is grown up
strong and healthy,
it bears fruit:

Apples.

When faith is grown up strong and healthy, it bears fruit too:

Joy

Self-control

Kindness

Humility

Love

Patience

Peace

Goodness

Faithfulness

When you pick an apple from a tree, you know it is an apple.

It looks like an apple.

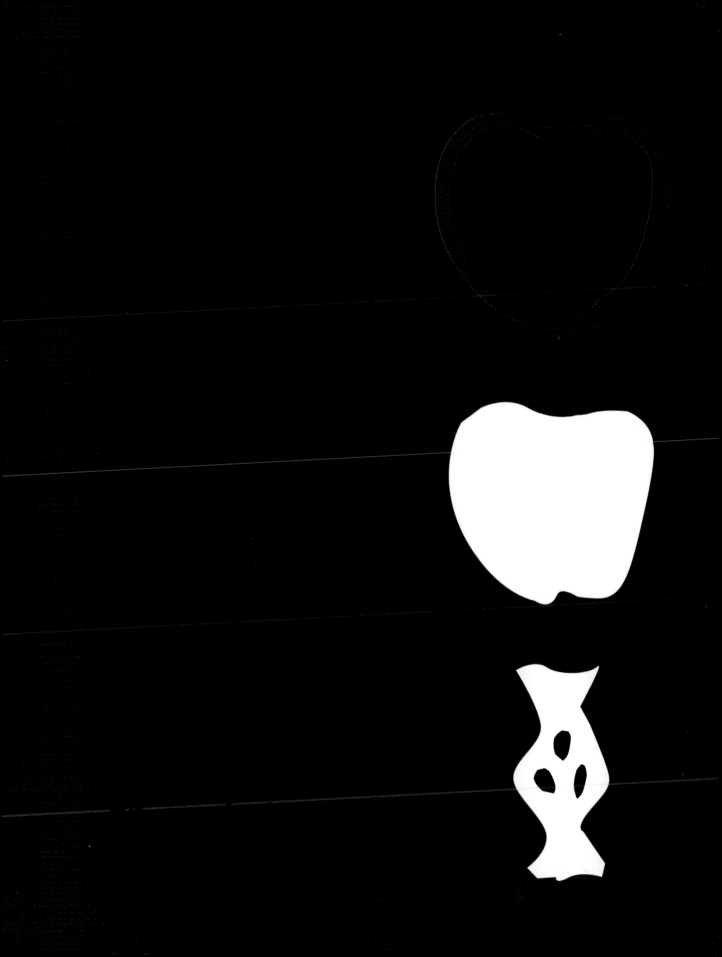

Although it has three parts,
You know you do not have three apples.

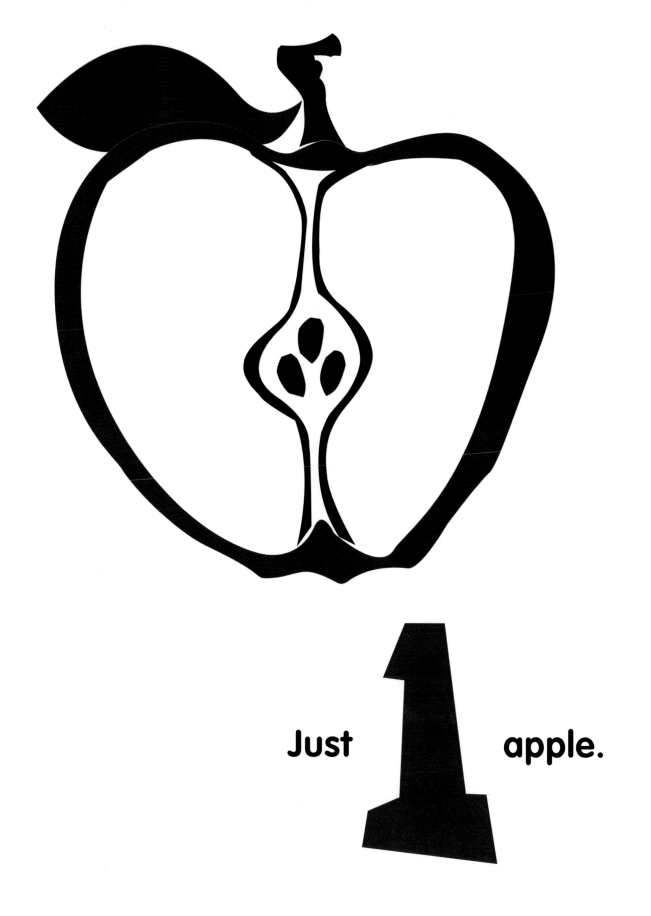

Just 1 apple.

If you have faith in the true God, you believe in

God the Father

God the Son

God the Holy Spirit

There are three Persons.

But there is only 1 true God.